POETRY ADVENTURES

IF IT RAINS PANCAKES

Haiku AND LANTERN POEMS

BRIAN P. CLEARY

ILLUSTRATIONS BY
ANDY ROWLAND

M MILLBROOK PRESS/MINNEAPOLIS

For Maryann,
Imani & Fatma
—BPC

For my little
pancake, Alice
—AR

Millbrook Press
A division of Lerner Publishing Group, Inc.
241 First Avenue North
Minneapolis, MN 55401 USA

For reading levels and more information, look up this title at www.lernerbooks.com.

Main body text set in Klepto ITC Std Regular 15/27.
Typeface provided by International Typeface Corp.

Library of Congress Cataloging-in-Publication Data

Cleary, Brian P., 1959–
    [Poems. Selections]
    If It Rains Pancakes : Haiku and Lantern Poems / by Brian P. Cleary ; illustrated by Andy Rowland.
        pages   cm. — (Poetry Adventures)
    ISBN 978-1-4677-1609-3 (lib. bdg. : alk. paper)
    ISBN 978-1-4677-2531-6 (eBook)
    I. Rowland, Andrew, 1962– ill. II. Title.
    PS3553.L39144I35 2014
    811'.54—dc23   2013018079

Manufactured in the United States of America
1 – DP – 12/31/13

TABLE OF CONTENTS

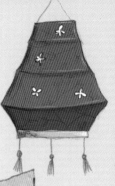

WHaT Is a HaiKu?

Haiku is a short, Japanese form of poetry that has been around for more than four hundred years. That's much longer than your teacher or your parents have even been alive! According to Japanese tradition, there are 17 sounds in each poem. These sounds are known in Japanese by a special term: *on*. It is pronounced like the English word *own* but a little faster. For our purposes, let's call those sounds syllables.

Each haiku has three lines. The first line has 5 syllables, the middle line has 7, and the final line has 5. Think of a haiku as a sandwich, with the 5-syllable lines as the bread and the 7-syllable line as the stuff in the middle! Traditionally, haiku have nature as their subject, and they often capture a specific moment. For this book, I've taken a broader approach to topics. You'll find poems about nature as well as about school, pets, pizza, pancakes, and more. I always like to say, "Poetry's not just a spectator sport," so try your hand at this ancient form, and be sure to have fun!

APRiL

Yellow tulips rise
as if they're awakening
from winter's slumber.

WATCH OUT

My pet pig, Betty,
in her full karate stance,
performs the "pork chop."

COLOR ME CONFUSED

Red always means stop.
Unless you're a bull—then it's
just the opposite.

Decisions

Spanish homework or
a nap? Compromise: we'll call
it a siesta.

OUTDOOR CONCERT

Wren chirps a chorus.

Frogs croak their steady bass line:

nature's symphony.

DRIFTING

Grandma's screened-in porch—
crickets croon their lullaby
as sleep summons me.

CITY OF BROTHERLY LUNCH

Philadelphia:

Birthplace of America

and tasty cheesesteaks.

DELISH

Cheese for Eloise,

Pepperoni for Tony.

I love pizza day.

YUMMY

When something's so good
you want to taste it again,
that's what burps are for.

Reflection

Sunset on the lake—
like a brilliant yellow road
to a sinking ball.

Autumn

Fall leaves crunch-crunching,
crisp air, warm clothes, and the sound
of the marching band.

WHAT IF?

If it rains pancakes,
I'll need no umbrella, just
syrup, fork, and plate.

SNOW(Y) DAY

Are the falling white
fluffy puffs enough to give
us the day off school?

RᴇVᴇRSᴀL

Noses smell. Feet run.
But the opposite also
is oftentimes true.

BᴀBY

Scream, pause, scream, pause, scream.
How can such a tiny mouth
create so much sound?

NATURE

Brown leaves, curled and dried.

Acorns; straw; and rich, brown dirt.

I should clean my room.

THE MIND

Memory is like

a room where tiny boxes

hold our yesterdays.

LUCKY DUCKS

Ducks walk, swim, and fly.

I walk. I swim a little.

But planes make me sick.

Haiku

When you've written one

without enough syllables,

you add words. Football.

ZZZZZZZZ

On the other side
of the pillow—that's where all
the best dreams are found.

WHaT Is
a LaNTeRN?

The lantern (sometimes spelled
lanturne) is another short, Japanese
form of poetry. The first line consists of
a 1-syllable noun (person, place, or thing).
That noun is the subject of the poem. The
following lines describe that subject—or as
the name *lantern* suggests, *shed light* on it.
Line 2 has 2 syllables. Line 3 has 3 syllables. Line
4 has 4. Line 5 goes back to 1 syllable. All lines are
centered on the page, so the finished poem roughly
resembles the shape of a Japanese lantern.

1 syllable ||||||| ||||⟹ Eggs ||||||||||||||||||||||

2 syllables |||||| |⟹ shelter |||||||||||||||||||||

3 syllables ||| ||⟹ within them ||||||||||||||||

4 syllables ||| ⟹ warmth and safety: ||||||||||||

1 syllable |||||||||||⟹ life. ||||||||||||||||||||

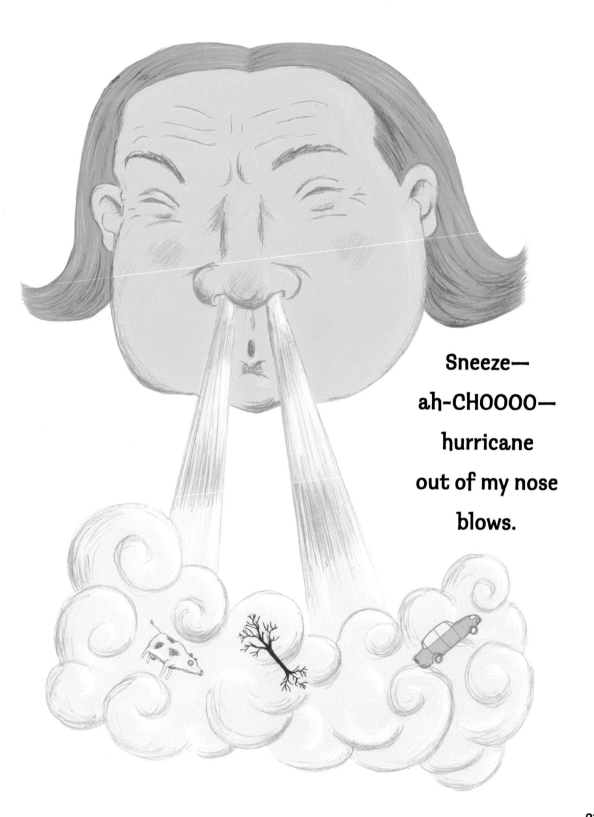

Sneeze—
ah-CHOOOO—
hurricane
out of my nose
blows.

Bees—
flying,
hardworking
honey makers—
buzz.

Cat:
"Feed me."
"Pet me too."
"Feed me. Pet me."
"Now."

Hug:
a gift
that is best
when you return
it.

Bed:
pillows
are twin clouds.
Stretch, read, doze, sleep.
Peace.

Stars
twinkling
in the dark:
angels winking
light.

Dawn:
rise, shine.
Tomorrow
is already
here.

Lunch:
cheese pool
with pasta
swimming in it.
Yum.

Slush—
gulping
icy treat.
Getting brain freeze.
Whoa.

Spring.
Yellows,
Blues, and greens.
Chirp, peck, peep, pop,
bloom.

Gum—
tasty
pink goodness.
Chomp, chomp, puff, puff . . .
POP!

Ball:
bouncy,
red and round.
You need to be
kicked.

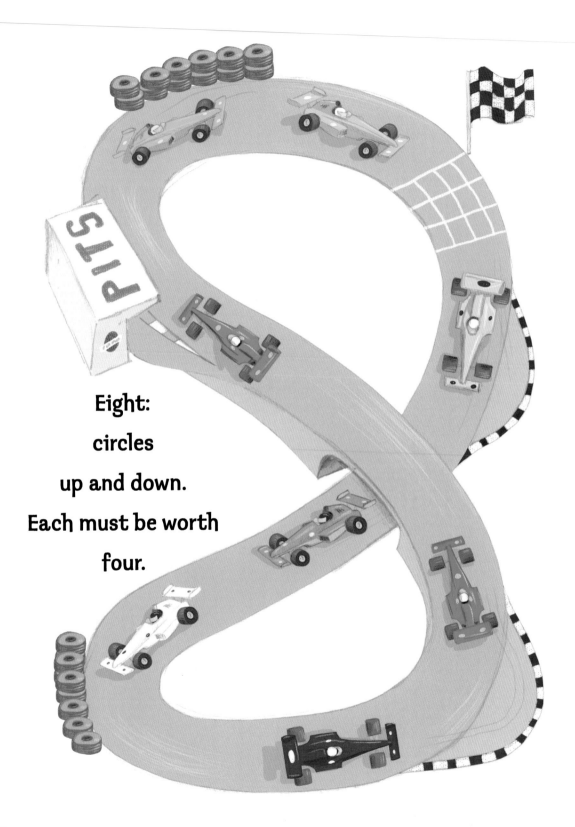

Eight:
circles
up and down.
Each must be worth
four.

Nap.
Awake
to teacher
still talking on.
Oops!

Bus
wheezes
to a stop.
Doors gasp open.
Home!

FURTHER READING

BOOKS

Cleary, Brian P. *Rainbow Soup: Adventures in Poetry.* Minneapolis: Carolrhoda Books, 2004.
Discover poems of all kinds in this entertaining collection.

Higgins, Nadia. *Henry and Hala Build a Haiku.* Chicago: Norwood House, 2011.
Check out this book for a refresher on how to make your own haiku.

Raczka, Bob. *Guyku: A Year of Haiku for Boys.* New York: Houghton Mifflin, 2010.
Boys and girls can enjoy these fun seasonal poems!

Rosen, Michael J. *The Hound Dog's Haiku and Other Poems for Dog Lovers.* Somerville, MA: Candlewick, 2011.
Pets and poetry make the perfect combination.

WEBSITES

Giggle Poetry
http://www.gigglepoetry.com
Find funny poems, poetry contests, and more on this activity-packed website.

Guyku
http://www.hmhbooks.com/guyku/index.html
After you've read Bob Raczka's book *Guyku (above),* check out more activities here.

Instant Poetry Forms
http://ettcweb.lr.k12.nj.us/forms/newpoem.htm
Make your own haiku and lantern poems! Follow the prompts, and this website will put your words into the right shapes.

Kenn Nesbitt's Poetry for Kids
http://www.poetry4kids.com
The poetry playground of Children's Poet Laureate Kenn Nesbitt is filled with funny poems and poetry books, games, contests, poetry lessons and activities, and lots more.